THIS BOOK BELONGS TO

CW00550611

SOUTHAMPTON FC

Name: _____   Age: _____

Favourite player: _____

2023/24

MY PREDICTIONS	ACTUAL
The Saints' final position:	
The Saints' top scorer:	
Championship winners:	
Championship top scorer:	
FA Cup winners:	
EFL Cup winners:	

Contributors: Peter Rogers, Sam Tighe.

A TWOCAN PUBLICATION

978-1-915571-57-1

£10

CONTENTS

THE CHAMPIONSHIP
SQUAD
2023/24

ALEX McCARTHY 1

POSITION: Goalkeeper **COUNTRY:** England **DOB:** 03/12/1989

Saints' longest-serving goalkeeper arrived from Crystal Palace in 2016 and has gone on to make more than 100 Premier League appearances for the club. McCarthy excelled in the 2017/18 campaign, helping the team survive in the top flight and picking up the Players' and Fans' Player of the Year awards that season. Capped once by England.

KYLE WALKER-PETERS 2

POSITION: Defender **COUNTRY:** English **DOB:** 13/04/1997

A versatile full-back capable of playing on both flanks, Walker-Peters came through the Tottenham Hotspur Academy and was in the Spurs squad that reached the 2019 Champions League final. An Under-20 World Cup winner, he made his senior international debut in 2022 despite facing competition from a host of world-class England right-backs.

RYAN MANNING

3

POSITION: **Defender**   COUNTRY: **Republic of Ireland**   DOB: **14/06/1996**

An adventurous attacking left-back, Manning starred under Russell Martin at Swansea, registering five goals and ten assists in the 2022/23 Championship campaign. His first two assists in a Saints shirt helped the team to a 2-1 victory over QPR, where Manning spent five years as a player following his arrival in England from Galway United in Ireland.

FLYNN DOWNES

4

POSITION: **Midfielder**   COUNTRY: **England**   DOB: **20/01/1999**

Another player with past experience under Martin, Downes spent the 2021/22 season at the Liberty Stadium after signing from Ipswich, where he progressed through the Academy. Joined Saints on loan from West Ham, the club he supported as a boy, where he was a member of the triumphant Europa Conference League squad.

JACK STEPHENS

5

POSITION: **Defender**   COUNTRY: **England**   DOB: **27/01/1994**

A ball-playing defender who fits the way Russell Martin wants to play, Stephens returned from a loan spell at Bournemouth with an uncertain future, but was soon succeeding James Ward-Prowse as captain. The Cornishman brought up 250 career appearances in the victory at Plymouth, the club where it all began.

MASON HOLGATE — 6

POSITION: **Defender**   COUNTRY: **England**   DOB: **22/10/1996**

Holgate played in the same Barnsley youth team as Saints teammate James Bree, and won the Young Player of the Year award at Oakwell. His performances earned a move to Everton aged 18, where he has played more than 100 times in the Premier League, and even captained the side. Can play as a central defender, right-back or in midfield.

ADAM ARMSTRONG — 9

POSITION: **Forward**   COUNTRY: **England**   DOB: **10/02/1997**

A boyhood Newcastle fan, Armstrong started his career at St James' Park and has played for the same three clubs as his idol, Alan Shearer. A prolific goalscorer at Championship level, he scored 46 goals in his last two seasons with Blackburn, and started Saints' promotion push in red-hot form. Won the Under-20 World Cup with England in 2017.

JOE ARIBO — 7

POSITION: **Defender**   COUNTRY: **Nigeria**   DOB: **21/10/1996**

Signed for Charlton from non-league Staines Town in 2015 and helped the Addicks win the League One Play-Offs in 2018/19, his final season with the club. Won the Scottish Premiership and Scottish Cup with Rangers, also scoring in the 2022 Europa League final, but the Glasgow giants fell to a heart-breaking penalty shoot-out defeat.

CHÉ ADAMS — 10

POSITION: **Forward**   COUNTRY: **Scotland**   DOB: **13/07/1996**

From non-league to the Premier League, Adams progressed through the divisions with a wholehearted, bustling style that has proved a handful for even the best defenders. Arrived at St Mary's following a 22-goal season with Birmingham in the Championship, and opened his Saints account with a spectacular long-range winner against Man City.

THE CHAMPIONSHIP
SQUAD
2023/24

ROSS STEWART — 11

POSITION: Forward **COUNTRY:** Scotland **DOB:** 11/07/1996

Arrived on transfer deadline day from Sunderland where he scored at a prolific rate, bagging 26 goals in the Mackems' League One promotion-winning campaign and ten in the Championship, despite missing more than half of the season with injury. Capped twice by Scotland in 2022, he stands at 6ft 2in tall, but possesses deceptive pace.

PAUL ONUACHU — 12

POSITION: Forward **COUNTRY:** Nigeria **DOB:** 28/05/1994

Signed in January 2023 after scoring at a prolific rate in the Belgian Pro League, Onuachu hit 17 goals in the first half of the season when Saints snapped him up on transfer deadline day from Genk. A towering presence at 6ft 7in tall, the centre-forward has 18 caps for Nigeria and is a teammate of Joe Aribo on the international stage.

THE CHAMPIONSHIP
SQUAD
2023/24

JOE LUMLEY — 13

POSITION: Goalkeeper **COUNTRY:** England **DOB:** 15/02/1995

Goalkeeper Lumley began his career at QPR, having been released by Tottenham as a teenager. He spent 11 years at Loftus Road, making 84 appearances for the club, whilst also being loaned out on eight occasions. Signed for Saints following a two-year spell with Middlesbrough, and spent the 2022/23 campaign on loan at Reading.

JAMES BREE — 14

POSITION: Defender **COUNTRY:** England **DOB:** 11/12/1997

Signed from Luton in January 2023, Bree was highly rated by Nathan Jones, his former boss at Kenilworth Road. The right-back has huge experience in the Championship, having played in the division for Barnsley, Aston Villa, Ipswich and Luton. Became Barnsley's second-youngest debutant at 16 years and 143 days old against QPR in 2014.

WILL
SMALLBONE
16

POSITION: Midfielder   **COUNTRY:** Republic of Ireland   **DOB:** 21/02/2000

An intelligent midfield player never flustered in possession, Smallbone returned to Saints following a season-long loan at Stoke in the Championship in the 2022/23 campaign, in which he also made his international debut for Republic of Ireland. Scored on his Saints debut as a 19-year-old in an FA Cup tie against Huddersfield in 2020.

STUART
ARMSTRONG
17

POSITION: Midfielder   **COUNTRY:** Scotland   **DOB:** 30/03/1992

An experienced Scotland international, Armstrong's debut for the Tartan Army was also the last of Russell Martin's 29 caps, as the pair briefly overlapped as teammates. A serial trophy winner with Celtic, the midfielder is a smooth ball carrier with a knack for scoring long-range goals. One of Saints' most creative players since his 2018 arrival.

SÉKOU
MARA
18

POSITION: Forward   **COUNTRY:** France   **DOB:** 30/07/2002

A French Under-21 international, Mara arrived from Bordeaux with bundles of potential, having broken into the first team as an 18-year-old. He showcased his talent with a defence-splitting pass to set up Kyle Walker-Peters to score a late equaliser against Leeds on his Premier League debut, and already has two goals against Man City to his name.

11

MOUSSA DJENEPO 19

POSITION: Midfielder   **COUNTRY:** Mali   **DOB:** 15/06/1998

Signed from Standard Liège in Belgium in 2019, Djenepo started his Saints career with a bang, scoring spectacular goals in Premier League wins at Brighton and Sheffield United. A hard-working and skilful winger, the Mali international has also featured as a wing-back and full-back on both flanks. Signed a three-year contract extension in 2022.

TAYLOR HARWOOD-BELLIS 20

POSITION: Defender   **COUNTRY:** England   **DOB:** 30/01/2002

Signed on a season-long loan from Manchester City, Harwood-Bellis arrived following a superb individual campaign. The centre-back, who has previous Championship experience with Blackburn and Stoke, was a mainstay of the Burnley side that won the title with 101 points, before captaining England Under-21s to European glory in the summer.

KAMALDEEN SULEMANA 20

POSITION: Forward   **COUNTRY:** Ghana   **DOB:** 15/02/2002

An explosive forward, Kamaldeen possesses an electrifying turn of pace that he uses to race in behind defences. Signed in January 2023 from French club Rennes, the Ghanaian showcased his potential with two goals against Liverpool in a thrilling 4-4 draw. Clocked at 35.7km/h, he was officially the fastest player at the Qatar World Cup.

CARLOS ALCARAZ 22

POSITION: Midfielder   **COUNTRY:** Argentina   **DOB:** 30/11/2002

A talented young midfielder with an eye for goal, Alcaraz quickly adapted to the Premier League following his January arrival from Racing Club in Argentina, despite having a limited grasp of English. Possesses tremendous timing with his late runs into the box and a fierce shot from distance. Scored the winner in the 2022 Argentinian Cup final.

SAMUEL EDOZIE 23

POSITION: **Midfielder**   COUNTRY: **England**   DOB: **28/01/2003**

An exciting player to watch, Edozie is an elusive dribbler, light on his feet and a headache for any full-back with his appetite to take risks in possession. One of four summer signings from Manchester City in 2022, the winger was initially used as an impact player off the bench, but enjoyed a run of starts in the Championship following relegation.

SHEA CHARLES 24

POSITION: **Midfielder**   COUNTRY: **Northern Ireland**   DOB: **05/11/2003**

Another former Man City youngster, Manchester-born Charles came through the City Academy, where he won two Premier League 2 titles, the latter as captain. Joined Saints in the summer of 2023 after making his senior debut under Pep Guardiola in the Premier League. A Northern Ireland international, he can play in midfield or at centre-back.

13

SOUTHAMPTON FC

RYAN FRASER   26

POSITION: Midfielder   **COUNTRY:** Scotland   DOB: 24/02/1994

Another of Russell Martin's former international teammates, Fraser made his Scotland debut in 2017. Standing at just 5ft 4in tall, the winger's low centre of gravity gives him explosive acceleration and a sharp change of direction. He played more than 200 games for Bournemouth before reuniting with his former boss, Eddie Howe, at Newcastle.

SAM AMO-AMEYAW   27

POSITION: Midfielder   **COUNTRY:** England   DOB: 18/07/2006

A hugely talented winger, Amo-Ameyaw arrived from Tottenham Hotspur as a 16-year-old in 2022. He helped Saints reach the FA Youth Cup semi-finals in his first year with the Under-18s, before being propelled into the first team as Saints' youngest Premier League debutant, aged 16 years and 314 days, against Liverpool on the season's final day.

JUAN LARIOS — 28

POSITION: **Defender**   COUNTRY: **Spain**   DOB: **12/01/2004**

A diminutive yet competitive full-back, Larios joined from Manchester City in 2022 along with former teammates Samuel Edozie, Gavin Bazunu and Roméo Lavia. A natural left-back, Larios has also played on the right side, but has seen his progress hampered by injuries. A Spanish youth international, the defender was previously on Barcelona's books.

TYLER DIBLING — 33

POSITION: **Forward**   COUNTRY: **England**   DOB: **12/03/2006**

An England youth international, Dibling played in the 2023 Under-17 European Championships. Possessing excellent dribbling and shooting skills, he scored a hat-trick of near identical goals in a Premier League 2 game at Newcastle in April 2022. He has since signed a professional contract until 2025 and made his first-team debut.

GAVIN BAZUNU — 31

POSITION: **Goalkeeper**   COUNTRY: **Republic of Ireland**   DOB: **20/02/2002**

A goalkeeper whose youth belies his experience, Bazunu has already racked up more than 100 appearances in English league football and established himself as Ireland's No 1. He spent time on loan with Rochdale and Portsmouth from Man City before joining Saints in 2022. Once saved a penalty from Cristiano Ronaldo in a World Cup qualifier.

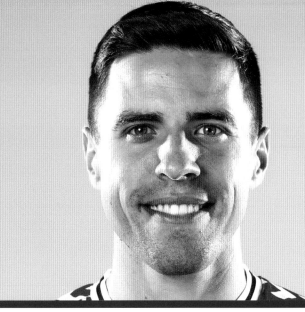

JAN BEDNAREK — 35

POSITION: **Defender**   COUNTRY: **Poland**   DOB: **12/04/1996**

An experienced international defender, Bednarek earned his 50th cap for Poland in 2023. Signed from Lech Poznań in his homeland in 2017, the centre-back scored on his Premier League debut against Chelsea, and has made more than 150 top-flight appearances for Saints. Spent the first half of the 2022/23 campaign on loan to Aston Villa.

SOUTHAMPTON WOMEN'S FC

Southampton Women finished sixth out of twelve teams in their debut season in the Barclays Women's Championship in 2022/23.

The players turned professional ahead of the campaign, allowing them to train and play full-time, and all home games were staged at St Mary's Stadium.

After a 2-0 defeat to Charlton Women on the opening day of the season, Marieanne Spacey-Cale's side went on a nine-game unbeaten run in the league which included four consecutive victories against Birmingham City Women (1-0), Sheffield United Women (1-0), Sunderland Women (1-0) and a 3-0 defeat of Coventry United.

Other notable league results for Saints included a 2-0 win over Crystal Palace, a 1-0 victory over London City Lionesses and a 1-1 draw at eventual Championship title-winners Bristol City as they recorded nine wins, six draws and just seven losses altogether in the league.

The Saints found the cup competitions more challenging. In the Women's FA Cup, they were knocked out by Bristol City in the third round (0-2) and finished bottom of Group E in the Conti Cup following a 2-0 defeat to Coventry United, 3-0 loss against Reading in front of 4,258 fans at St Mary's and 1-0 defeat to Tottenham Hotspur - again in front of a good crowd of 2,725 in Southampton.

At the inaugural 'On Her Side' awards in May 2023, Kayla Rendell - who played in all but one of Saints' league matches - was voted Barclays Women's Championship Goalkeeper of the Season and Milly Mott was named the Women's Championship Rising Star for her contribution in 20 league appearances in 2022/23. Spacey-Cale was awarded second place in the Manager of the Season vote.

At the club's awards, Saints fans voted Laura Rafferty's strike against Lewes in August 2022 their Women's Goal of the Season.

The side got their 2023/24 Women's Championship campaign off to a great start with a 4-1 away victory against Lewes Women thanks to goals from Katie Wilkinson, Sophia Pharaoh, Ella Morris and Molly Pike.

MARIEANNE SPACEY-CALE

RIGHT: MILLY MOTT
& GOALKEEPER KAYLA RENDELL

WOMEN'S CHAMPIONSHIP
SQUAD
2023/24

KAYLA RENDELL — 1

POSITION: Goalkeeper   **COUNTRY:** England   **DOB:** 29/06/2001

A product of the academy, Rendell was a key player in Saints' rise through the women's pyramid. Keeping nine clean sheets and making 89 saves in her debut season in the Barclays Women's Championship, Rendell received Fans' Player of the Year as well as making the shortlist for Save of the Season across the entire league.

ELLA MORRIS — 2

POSITION: Defender   **COUNTRY:** England   **DOB:** 23/09/2002

An attacking-minded defender, Morris is another player who has progressed through the academy to become a first-team stalwart. A player with pace to burn, Morris scored Saints' first-ever goal in the Barclays Women's Championship as the side left it late to draw 2-2 with Lewes and has seen her performances rewarded with Young Lionesses call-ups.

MILLY MOTT 3

POSITION: **Defender**   COUNTRY: **England**   DOB: **28/11/2003**

A conventional right-back, Mott has made the position her own over the past few seasons. Providing excellent strength in defence, Mott was an ever-present player in the side that achieved promotion to the Barclays Women's Championship, and started nearly every game in the 2022/23 season making 22 appearances.

LUCIA KENDALL 4

POSITION: **Midfielder**   COUNTRY: **England**   DOB: **20/05/2004**

Another Saints academy product, Kendall played a key role in the side's promotion to the Barclays Women's Championship in 2021/22, providing 22 goals in 27 appearances. Despite injury at the beginning of the debut Championship season, Kendall made her comeback in October 2022, scoring against Birmingham City at Snows Stadium to give Saints all three points.

ROSIE PARNELL 5

POSITION: **Defender**   COUNTRY: **England**   DOB: **04/06/1994**

Named captain for the 2023/24 season, centre-back Parnell is a rock at the heart of Saints' defence. Spending time at the Southampton FC academy as a young player, Parnell moved away before making her return to the club in 2019. Making 22 appearances in the debut Women's Championship season, Parnell is characterised by her strong aerial presence and ability to pull off big tackles in key moments.

LAURA RAFFERTY 6

POSITION: **Defender** COUNTRY: **Northern Ireland** DOB: **29/04/1996**

Northern Ireland international Rafferty has been a key player in Marieanne Spacey-Cale's side since her arrival for the 2021/22 season. A vocal presence in the Saints back-line Rafferty made 32 appearances during the promotion winning season and 11 during the side's 2022/23 debut Championship season, scoring the fans' Goal of the Season.

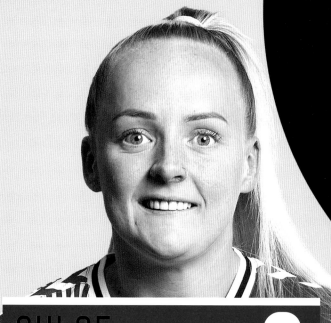

CHLOE PEPLOW 8

POSITION: **Midfielder** COUNTRY: **Scotland** DOB: **03/12/1998**

Joining Saints on loan from Reading FC Women in January 2023, Peplow was quick to make an impact in the centre of midfield. A strong, technical player, Peplow made six appearances during the second half of the 2022/23 season, becoming a fan favourite. Signing a permanent contract with the club in the summer transfer window, Peplow was a consistent starter during pre-season.

LEXI LLOYD-SMITH 7

POSITION: **Midfielder** COUNTRY: **England** DOB: **05/03/2003**

Another incoming ahead of a debut Championship season, Lloyd-Smith provides a versatile option in attack, playing either through the middle or on the wing. Making 15 appearances during the 2022/23 campaign, Lloyd-Smith scored a memorable brace against Crystal Palace at Selhurst Park.

KATIE WILKINSON 9

POSITION: **Forward** COUNTRY: **England** DOB: **05/11/1994**

Top goalscorer during the 2022/23 season with seven goals, Wilkinson was another addition ahead of Saints' debut season in the Barclays Women's Championship. Scoring an impressive hat-trick against her old side Coventry United at St Mary's in November 2022, her first goal came less than 20 seconds into the game. Wilkinson also scored the first goal of Saints' 2023/24 season, netting in the sides 4-1 win away at Lewes FC.

SQUAD

2023/24

RIANNA DEAN **10**

POSITION: **Forward**   COUNTRY: **England**   DOB: **21/10/1998**

Joining from fellow Barclays Women's Championship side Crystal Palace, Dean provides another exciting attacking option for Marieanne Spacey-Cale. Boasting experience with Arsenal, Tottenham Hotspur and Liverpool, Dean also made appearances for a number of England Youth sides, her last call-up coming for Mo Marley's U21s in 2020.

MEGAN WYNNE **11**

POSITION: **Midfielder**   COUNTRY: **Wales**   DOB: **21/01/1993**

A Welsh international, Wynne joined Saints ahead of their 2022/23 debut in the Barclays Women's Championship. Predominantly playing as a winger, Wynne is known for her speed and physicality, providing an excellent option in pressing games and made 20 appearances for Saints in the 2022/23 season.

21

SQUAD

2023/24

SOPHIA PHAROAH **12**

POSITION: **Forward** COUNTRY: **England** DOB: **11/09/2000**

Another player who spent the early part of their career at the Southampton FC academy, Pharoah is one of Marieanne Spacey-Cale's attacking and wide options. Scoring the goal against Wolverhampton Wanderers that secured promotion to the Championship, Pharoah was injured for much of the 2022/23 season, scoring one goal. Pharoah opened her goalscoring account for the 2023/24 season with a header in the opening game against Lewes.

MOLLY PIKE **14**

POSITION: **Midfielder** COUNTRY: **England** DOB: **22/01/2001**

An addition from Barclays Women's Super League Leicester City ahead of the 2023/24 season, Pike has been an exciting addition to Marieanne Spacey-Cale's side. Free-scoring in pre-season, Pike made her intentions clear, scoring on her competitive debut against Lewes in a 4-1 win at The Dripping Pan on the opening day of the 2023/24 season.

EMMA THOMPSON 16

POSITION: **Forward**   COUNTRY: **England**   DOB: **21/02/2004**

One of the youngest players in the squad, Thompson joined from Chelsea FC in the summer 2023 transfer window. Described as a 'classic number nine', Thompson made a number of appearances for the senior side at Chelsea, also leading the scoring for their academy side during the 2021/22 season, before joining Lewes FC on loan for the subsequent Barclays Women's Championship season.

IZZY MILNE 18

POSITION: **Defender**   COUNTRY: **England**   DOB: **08/02/2005**

Joining Saints from Chelsea FC's academy in the 2023 summer transfer window, Milne provides another left-footed option in the defensive line. Coming on as both a centre back and a left back in pre-season outings and making her debut in the opening game of the 2023/24 season at Lewes, Milne is a versatile player who was quick to mention her personal development when discussing her move to the south coast.

EMILY KRAFT 17

POSITION: **Forward**   COUNTRY: **Ireland**   DOB: **18/02/2002**

Joining Saints in the 2023 summer transfer window, the German-Irish Kraft is another addition to a strong forward line. Spending the 2022/23 season at Lewes, and scoring against Saints at St Mary's, Kraft spent her career up until that point at German side FFC Frankfurt. Kraft represented Germany up until U16 level before making the switch to Ireland, receiving her first senior call-up in 2019.

ALICE GRIFFITHS 19

POSITION: **Midfielder**   COUNTRY: **Wales**   DOB: **22/01/2001**

Another Welsh international, Griffiths provides a versatile and composed head in midfield. A master at ball recovery, Griffiths joined halfway through the 2021/22 promotion-winning season. Growing into the developing first-team side, the midfielder made 21 appearances during the 2022/23 league campaign and has cemented her place in the centre of midfield.

JEMMA PURFIELD 21

POSITION: **Defender**   COUNTRY: **England**   DOB: **21/02/1997**

A left-footed addition in the 2023 summer transfer window, Purfield offers Barclays Women's Super League experience to Saints' squad. Boasting stints at Liverpool, Bristol City and Leicester City, Purfield's set-piece aptitude makes her a tricky player to deal with when driving forward from defence.

ATLANTA PRIMUS 20

POSITION: **Forward**   COUNTRY: **Jamaica**   DOB: **21/04/1997**

A summer addition ahead of the 2023/24 Barclays Women's Championship season, Primus spent her off-season with Jamaica at the FIFA Women's World Cup. An attacking-minded midfielder, Primus helped the Reggae Girlz to their first-ever World Cup point.

BETH HOWARD 22

POSITION: **Goalkeeper**   COUNTRY: **England**   DOB: **06/06/1995**

One of Saints' January signings during the 2022/23 season, Howard made her debut against Coventry United at the Butts Park Arena, keeping a clean sheet. A commanding presence in her area, Howard provides a strong, experienced partner to keeper Kayla Rendell and made a number of appearances in the 2023/24 pre-season campaign.

SQUAD

2023/24

MEGAN COLLETT **23**

POSITION: **Defender**   COUNTRY: **England**   DOB: **11/07/2005**

Another of Saints' breakthrough academy players, Collett emerged as a first-team option during the 2021/22 promotion winning season. Making the wing-back role her own, Collett made 21 appearances during the debut 2022/23 Barclays Women's Championship season, and started in the first game of the new 2023/24 campaign. She has also received call-ups to the Young Lionesses.

PAIGE PEAKE **24**

POSITION: **Defender**   COUNTRY: **England**   DOB: **03/08/2002**

Joining from promotion rivals Ipswich Town ahead of the 2022/23 Barclays Women's Championship, Peake has become a key member of the Saints side. A strong aerial presence in the centre of the back-line, the defender combines set-piece prowess with game-reading ability. Peake scored a memorable injury-time penalty winner against promotion hopefuls London City Lionesses at Pride Park.

ONE OF THE HARDEST THINGS TO DO IN FOOTBALL IS TO STICK THE BALL IN THE BACK OF THE NET.

NOT LEAST BECAUSE THERE ARE USUALLY ELEVEN OTHER PLAYERS TRYING TO STOP YOU DOING JUST THAT!

SHOOTING
FROM
DISTANCE

Good service is obviously important, and a good understanding with your striking partner is also vital, but when it comes to spectacular strikes, practice is the key to hitting a consistently accurate and powerful shot and to developing the timing and power required.

EXERCISE

A small-sided pitch is set up with two 18-yard boxes put together, but the corners of the pitch are cut off as shown in the diagram. There are five players per team, including goalkeepers, but only one player is allowed in the opponent's half.

The aim of the drill is to work a shooting opportunity when you have the ball, with the likely chance being to shoot from outside your opponent's penalty area, from distance. The teams take it in turns to release the ball into play from their own 'keeper - usually by rolling out to an unmarked player.

18 YDS

KEY FACTORS

1. **Attitude to shooting - be positive, have a go!**
2. **Technique - use laces, hit through the ball.**
3. **Do not sacrifice accuracy for power.**
4. **Wide angle shooting - aim for the far post.**
5. **Always follow up for rebounds!**

SOCCER
SKILLS

The size of the pitch can be reduced for younger players, and it should be noted that these junior players should also be practicing with a size 4 or even a size 3 ball, depending on their age.

22

CARLOS
ALCARAZ

DAZZLING
DEFENDERS

FRANCIS BENALI, JOSÉ FONTE AND VIRGIL VAN DIJK WERE ALL GREAT SAINTS DEFENDERS. CONTINUING THAT PROUD TREND IS CURRENT SAINTS STAR JACK STEPHENS.

Fonte became an instant fan favourite when he left Championship side Crystal Palace for a Southampton side sitting one division lower. He believed he could reach the Premier League quicker from the south coast - and he was right.

The Portuguese was a key player in back-to-back promotions in 2011 and 2012, then helped establish the Saints as a consistent top-tier presence, eventually being given the armband in 2014.

His reading of the game was superb and he was titanic in the air, contributing a healthy 15 goals over seven great years at the club.

Born in Southampton, schooled in Southampton and, barring a brief loan spell at Nottingham Forest that helped him find his feet in the professional game, a football career spent solely in Southampton. It's the stuff of legend.

Francis Benali is beloved by the fanbase and for good reason, he's one of them. He achieved every fan's dream of pulling on the shirt and zipping about the pitch. He played an industrious role from left-back, making big blocks and crucial clearances.

His one, single goal in a Saints shirt, a looping header from a set piece, sparked truly epic celebrations in the stands.

FRANCIS BENALI

DATE OF BIRTH:	December 30, 1968
PLACE OF BIRTH:	Southampton
NATIONALITY:	England
SAINTS APPEARANCES:	373
SAINTS GOALS:	1
SAINTS DEBUT:	October 1, 1988

Southampton 0-0 Derby County (First Division)

JOSÉ FONTE

DATE OF BIRTH:	December 22, 1983
PLACE OF BIRTH:	Penafiel, Portugal
NATIONALITY:	Portuguese
SAINTS APPEARANCES:	288
SAINTS GOALS:	15
SAINTS DEBUT:	October 16, 2010

Millwall 1-1 Southampton (League One)

Virgil van Dijk's stay on the south coast was not the longest, but that's only because he was so incredibly good, Liverpool saw fit to spend a then-world record £75 million in order to make him a part of their squad.

His incredible calm and poise filtered through the rest of the team. His strong leadership and organisational skills lifted the level of those around him. Far from all-action, he read the game so well he was rarely forced into defensive heroics.

At Liverpool he went on to win league and European titles, cementing his status as part of the game's elite.

VIRGIL VAN DIJK

DATE OF BIRTH: July 8, 1991

PLACE OF BIRTH: Breda, Netherlands

NATIONALITY: Dutch

SAINTS APPEARANCES: 80

SAINTS GOALS: 7

SAINTS DEBUT: September 12, 2015
West Bromwich Albion 0-0 Southampton (Premier League)

JACK STEPHENS

DATE OF BIRTH: January 27, 1994

PLACE OF BIRTH: Torpoint, England

NATIONALITY: English

SAINTS APPEARANCES: 151*

SAINTS GOALS: 6*

SAINTS DEBUT: January 7, 2012
Coventry City 1-2 Southampton (FA Cup)

*AS AT THE END OF THE 2022/23 SEASON

Jack Stephens joined Southampton over a decade ago and, in between various loan moves, has racked up over 150 appearances for the club to date.

He spent the 2022/23 season with AFC Bournemouth, but has now returned to play a key role as captain with the Saints as they seek to win promotion back to the Premier League at the first attempt.

His comfort on the ball and excellent threaded forward passes have always been appreciated on the south coast and should be particularly effective in this coming season, given new manager Russell Martin counts this skillset as pivotal in his tactical setup.

SAMUEL
EDOZIE

23

FOOTY

ALL OF THESE FOOTY PHRASES ARE HIDDEN IN THE GRID, EXCEPT FOR ONE …BUT CAN YOU WORK OUT WHICH ONE? ANSWERS ON PAGE 62

PHRASES

```
C A E S W Y V Y B H U G N U R Y M M U D
V U Q I D E R B Y D A Y O L U R T S S U
K F A D J L G T X T F C B E I A K C F P
I B H E O T L P Z R V N M W O J I R Y A
C M O F F S I D E R U L E E D S P E Y H
M E R U E I J R D E D A Q G S H L A X C
R X E R N H A T T R I C K O I L A M R T
E I Y O W W S L S N O W R S O Z Y E Y A
D C A A Z L W S J K T K Y V K B M R T M
A A L P X A U Y H M I D F I E D A R O E
E N P T K N F W G C P L J K A M K N L H
H W E J A I L O K H A O F O H I E C G T
G A M E O F T W O H A L V E S T R N U F
N V A I A H E S L F J D U A O I U O T O
I E G B I C L A S S A C T U P F G E V N
V D G O A E E U C K S S C Y W U L Q L A
I R I R Q G M N S A C H G H D O S F G M
D V B A C K O F T H E N E T Z P X B N A
```

Back of the Net	**Diving Header**	**Half Volley**	**Offside Rule**
Big Game Player	**Dugout**	**Hat-trick**	**One-touch**
Brace	**Dummy Run**	**Keepie Uppie**	**Playmaker**
Class Act	**Final Whistle**	**Man of the Match**	**Scissor Kick**
Derby Day	**Game of Two Halves**	**Mexican Wave**	**Screamer**

THE WALL PASS

With teams being very organised in modern football, it can be very difficult to break them down and create scoring opportunities. One of the best ways to achieve this is by using the 'wall pass', otherwise known as the quick one-two.

EXERCISE

In a non-pressurised situation, involving four players, A carries the ball forward towards a static defender (in this case a cone) and before reaching the defender, plays the ball to B before running around the opposite side to receive the one-touch return pass. A then delivers the ball safely to C who then repeats the exercise returning the ball to D, and in this way the exercise continues. Eventually a defender can be used to make the exercise more challenging, with all players being rotated every few minutes.

The exercise can progress into a five-a-side game, the diagram below shows how additional players (W) on the touchline can be used as 'walls' with just one touch available to help the man in possession of the ball.

Each touchline player can move up and down the touchline, but not enter the pitch - they can also play for either team.

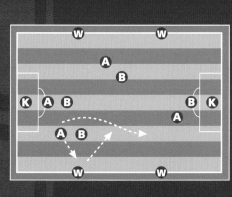

KEY FACTORS

1. Look to commit the defender before passing - do not play the ball too early.
2. Pass the ball firmly and to feet.
3. Accelerate past defender after passing.
4. Receiver (B) make themselves available for the pass.
5. B delivers a return pass, weighted correctly, into space.

SOCCER SKILLS

If done correctly, this is a tactic which is extremely difficult to stop, but needs teamwork and communication between the two attacking players.

5

ROSIE
PARNELL

A-Z

A

What nationality is Watford goalkeeper Daniel Bachmann?

A

B

Which team won the Sky Bet Championship title in 2022/23?

B

C

Which Premier League club reappointed their former manager as interim boss in March 2023?

C

D

Which League One side play their home matches at Pride Park?

D

E

What nationality is Liverpool's sensational striker Mohamed Salah?

E

F

Which country knocked England out of the FIFA World Cup finals in 2022?

F

34

Which famous football ground is due to host its final fixture in 2024?

G

 H Which club did Neil Warnock lead to Championship survival in 2022/23?

H

 I Which country did England defeat 6-2 in their opening game of the FIFA 2022 World Cup finals?

I

 J Aston Villa winger Leon Bailey plays internationally for which country?

J

K What is the name of Premier League new boys Luton Town's home ground?

K

L Can you name the Ipswich Town striker who netted 17 League One goals in the Tractor Boys' 2022/23 promotion-winning season?

L

M Which Championship club boasted the division's top scorer in 2022/23?

M

ANSWERS ON PAGE 62

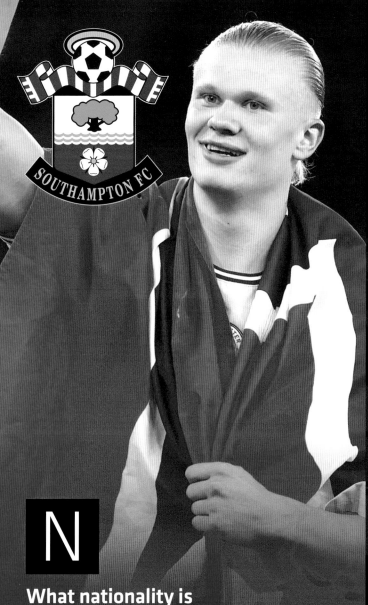

SOUTHAMPTON FC

Q Can you name the country that hosted the FIFA 2022 World Cup finals?

Q

R Which Spanish side did Manchester City defeat in last season's UEFA Champions League semi-final?

R

S Which team knocked Premier League champions Manchester City out of the Carabao Cup last season?

S

N

What nationality is Manchester City's ace marksman Erling Haaland?

N

O Can you name the former Premier League team that will compete in the National League in 2023/24?

O

P Which international striker ended five seasons with Norwich City in May 2023?

P

T Which full-back left Huddersfield Town to join Nottingham Forest ahead of their return to the Premier League in the summer of 2022?

T

U Can you name Brighton's German forward who joined the Seagulls in January 2022?

U

V Can you name the former England striker who has hit over 100 Premier League goals for Leicester City?

V

W Can you name the goalkeeper who got his name on the scoresheet last season in a Championship fixture?

W

X Can you name the Portuguese international defender who played in the Premier League with Everton, Liverpool & Middlesbrough?

X

Y At which club did Leeds United's Luke Ayling make his league debut?

Y

Z Which Dutch international midfielder played Premier League football for Chelsea, Middlesbrough and Liverpool in the 2000s?

Z

A-Z
PART TWO

KYLE
WALKER-PETERS

DESIGN A
FOOTY BOOT

Design a brilliant new footy boot
for the Saints squad!

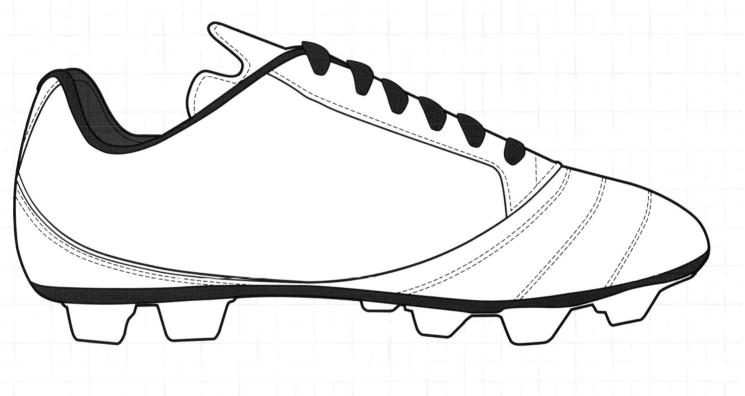

MIDFIELD MAESTROS

MATT LE TISSIER, ADAM LALLANA AND JAMES WARD-PROWSE WERE ALL REAL CREATORS AND SCORERS IN THE SAINTS MIDFIELD. CONTINUING THAT PROUD TREND IS CURRENT MAESTRO WILL SMALLBONE.

Adam Lallana made the step from academy to first team during the club's darkest hour, as it was relegated to the third tier of football and came close to going out of business.

The fact he was able to blossom into a stunning midfield playmaker despite this chaotic backdrop is testament to his ability and character.

Lallana looked a class above in the lower divisions, forming a great partnership with striker Rickie Lambert, which helped Saints back to the Premier League. His close control, footwork and mazy dribbling consistently bamboozled defenders as he created and scored goals in abundance.

Matt Le Tissier, the man who sometimes looked as if he was having a Goal of the Season competition with himself, brought joy and elation to Southampton fans for 16 years.

From looping long range chip shots, to thunderbolts steered into the top corner, to inch-perfect penalties, Le Tissier never stopped inventing ways to score and ways to entertain, his genius always shone through.

He turned down multiple big offers to move away from the club in order to stay loyal, and in 2000 he became the first midfielder in Premier League history to reach 100 goals in the competition.

MATT LE TISSIER

DATE OF BIRTH:	October 14, 1968
PLACE OF BIRTH:	St Peter Port
NATIONALITY:	English
SAINTS APPEARANCES:	435
SAINTS GOALS:	166
SAINTS DEBUT:	August 30, 1986

Norwich City 4 Southampton 3 (Division One)

ADAM LALLANA

DATE OF BIRTH:	August 23, 2006
PLACE OF BIRTH:	St Albans
NATIONALITY:	English
SAINTS APPEARANCES:	265
SAINTS GOALS:	60
SAINTS DEBUT:	August 23, 2006

Southampton 5 Yeovil Town 2 (League Cup)

Clocking over 400 appearances for his boyhood club, James Ward-Prowse secured legendary status at Southampton before he had even turned 28 years old, a rare and incredible feat.

Fans have watched him mature from unassuming yet silky passer to gritty, determined leader and set piece master. He ended the 2022/23 season just one free-kick away from equalling David Beckham's Premier League record and there's little that doubt he'll surpass that tally in the coming years.

A calm and measured face of the club, Ward-Prowse is beloved by the terraces and respected by all in the sport, regardless of allegiance.

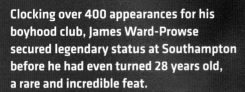

JAMES WARD-PROWSE

DATE OF BIRTH:	November 1, 1994
PLACE OF BIRTH:	Portsmouth
NATIONALITY:	English
SAINTS APPEARANCES:	409
SAINTS GOALS:	55
SAINTS DEBUT:	October 25, 2011

Crystal Palace 2 Southampton 0 (League Cup)

WILL SMALLBONE

DATE OF BIRTH:	February 21, 2000
PLACE OF BIRTH:	Basingstoke
NATIONALITY:	English
SAINTS APPEARANCES:	20*
SAINTS GOALS:	1*
SAINTS DEBUT:	January 4, 2020

Southampton 2 Huddersfield Town 0 (FA Cup)

*AS AT THE END OF THE 2022/23 SEASON

Rarely are footballing career paths simple, but finally, at 23 years of age, Will Smallbone is ready to take up a prominent role for the club he's been with since 2008.

Will had to overcome serious obstacles in the last few years, as in 2021 he tore his ACL and was diagnosed with alopecia, a combination which he admits hit his confidence levels hard.

But now, after a loan at Stoke City in which he grew as a person, he's ready to take command of Southampton's midfield as they hunt promotion back to the Premier League.

hummel

CLASSIC
FAN'TASTIC

Sammy Saint is hiding in the crowd in five different places as Saints fans celebrate winning the Johnstone's Paint Trophy at Wembley in 2010.

Can you find all five?

ANSWERS ON PAGE 62

16 WILL SMALLBONE

SOUTHAMPTON FC

Can you figure out which football is the real one in each of these photos?

WHICH...

...BALL

ANSWERS ON PAGE 62

45

3

RYAN
MANNING

SPOT...

...THE DIFFERENCE

ANSWERS ON PAGE 62

Can you find the eight differences between these two celebration photos?

SOUTHAMPTON FC

BEHIND THE

CAN YOU IDENTIFY EVERY ONE OF THESE SAINTS STARS...

BADGE

...HIDDEN BEHIND OUR BEAUTIFUL BADGE?

A

B

C

48

D

E

F

G

H

ADAM
ARMSTRONG

HAVE FUN COLOURING IN
THIS PICTURE OF SAINTS STAR

ADAM
ARMSTRONG

TRUE
COLOURS

STUNNING STRIKERS

MICK CHANNON, JAMES BEATTIE AND RICKIE LAMBERT WERE ALL ACE MARKSMEN FOR THE SAINTS. LOOKING TO FOLLOW IN THEIR FOOTSTEPS IS CURRENT STRIKER ADAM ARMSTRONG.

A symbol of Southampton's long Premier League stay in the early noughties, James Beattie grew from young prospect to feared goalscorer in front of The Dell's watching eyes.

After a settling in period he found his feet at the turn of the millennium, consistently hitting double figures in goals, then in 2002-03 scored an incredible 23 times, making him the highest-scoring Englishman in the division. During that time he led the Saints to an FA Cup final and made his England bow too.

His form dipped after that and moved on in early 2005 to Everton for a £6m fee—but never truly found his best levels again.

They say never go back, but Mick Channon ignored that old adage and enjoyed two successful spells with Southampton between 1965 and 1982.

In his first spell he scored at a rate of knots despite the club enduring a tough time overall. He stayed with the Saints following relegation to the Second Division in 1974, paving the way for him to become a key figure in the club's fairytale 1976 FA Cup win, beating Manchester United in the final.

After a brief spell with Manchester City, he returned south in 1979 to play three more years and score just shy of 30 more goals for the club.

MICK CHANNON

DATE OF BIRTH:	November 28, 1948
PLACE OF BIRTH:	Orcheston
NATIONALITY:	English
SAINTS APPEARANCES:	608
SAINTS GOALS:	228
SAINTS DEBUT:	April 11, 1966
	Southampton 2 Bristol City 2 (Division Two)

JAMES BEATTIE

DATE OF BIRTH:	February 27, 1978
PLACE OF BIRTH:	Lancaster
NATIONALITY:	English
SAINTS APPEARANCES:	233
SAINTS GOALS:	76
SAINTS DEBUT:	August 16, 1998
	Southampton 1-2 Liverpool (Premier League)

A goal machine at three different levels, Rickie Lambert was one of the great stories emanating from Southampton's drop into League One a decade and a half ago.

A powerful and physically dominant striker, he breached the fabled 20-goal mark three seasons in a row as he powered Southampton to two promotions, landing them back into the Premier League.

Excellent in the air and a pure striker of the ball, he transitioned to the top level seamlessly, scoring 15 and 13 goals in two campaigns before winning a dream move to his boyhood club Liverpool.

RICKIE LAMBERT

DATE OF BIRTH: February 16, 1982

PLACE OF BIRTH: Kirkby

NATIONALITY: England

SAINTS APPEARANCES: 235

SAINTS GOALS: 117

SAINTS DEBUT: August 11, 2009
Southampton 2-0 Northampton Town (League Cup)

ADAM ARMSTRONG

DATE OF BIRTH: February 10, 1997

PLACE OF BIRTH: Newcastle

NATIONALITY: English

SAINTS APPEARANCES: 67*

SAINTS GOALS: 5*

SAINTS DEBUT: August 14,2021
Everton 3-1 Southampton (Premier League)

*AS AT THE END OF THE 2022/23 SEASON

As he enters his third year with the club, there's real optimism that we're about to see the best of Adam Armstrong in a Southampton shirt.

Last time he set foot in the Championship he scored 28 goals for Blackburn Rovers in 2020/21, singling him out as a top marksman at this level, and prompting Saints to buy him.

His remarkable pace, clever movements and instinctive shooting make him a natural threat on goal. All he needs is for the ball to be threaded through for him and he's off, bearing down on goal and ready to pull the trigger.

REWIND

THREE GREAT SAINTS MATCHES FROM 2023

Sheffield Wednesday 1
Southampton 2

SKY BET CHAMPIONSHIP · AUGUST 4, 2023

Southampton made a winning start to life back in the Championship in August 2023 after 11 consecutive seasons in the Premier League.

Adam Armstrong gave Saints an eighth-minute lead as they visited Hillsborough on the opening night of the 2023/24 league season A spectacular left-footed shot from Nathan Tella took the smallest of flicks off his back to end up in the back of the Owls net. Lee Gregory equalised on 54 minutes but Ché Adams secured the three points for Saints with three minutes of the 90 remaining when he finished from a James Ward-Prowse cut-back.

Southampton 4
Norwich City 4

SKY BET CHAMPIONSHIP · AUGUST 12, 2023

Josh Sargent put Norwich City 1-0 up after seven minutes of an enthralling Championship encounter at St Mary's. Jan Bednarek levelled and an Adam Armstrong penalty put Saints 2-1 up before Gabriel equalised for the visitors on 23 minutes.

A Jonathan Rowe strike in first-half stoppage time saw the Canaries 3-2 up at the break. In the second half, Ché Adams' second goal of the season restored parity before Christian Fassnacht broke Southampton hearts with a late goal that looked like giving the visitors all three points. But Saints had other ideas. Their efforts were rewarded in the seventh minute of stoppage time when Armstrong stuck home his second penalty of the afternoon.

Plymouth Argyle 1
Southampton 2

SKY BET CHAMPIONSHIP · AUGUST 19, 2023

Southampton's unbeaten start to the 2023/24 campaign continued at Home Park against Championship new boys Plymouth Argyle.

Nathan Tella put Russell Martin's side one-nil up four minutes into the second half, but Ryan Hardie levelled for the Pilgrims less than two minutes later. With the game seemingly destined for a draw, Saints displayed their canny knack of scoring late goals once again as Ché Adams popped up with the winner in the fourth minute of stoppage time.

FAST FORWARD

...AND THREE BIG CHAMPIONSHIP ENCOUNTERS TO COME IN 2024...

Norwich City
VERSUS
Southampton

SKY BET CHAMPIONSHIP · JANUARY 1, 2024

The calendar year of 2024 begins with a New Year's Day trip to Carrow Road. Norwich City are a club Saints boss Russell Martin knows well having played 309 matches for the Norfolk side between 2009 and 2018.

As mentioned in this feature, the corresponding fixture between the two sides earlier in the 2023/24 Championship season was an absolute cracker. With Saints and the Canaries both attack-minded teams, a high-scoring match could be the cards once again on New Year's Day.

Southampton
VERSUS
Stoke City

SKY BET CHAMPIONSHIP · APRIL 29, 2024

The visit of Stoke City to St Mary's concludes a busy month for Saints, who face no less that six Championship matches in April 2024.

Russell Martin's side face trips to Ipswich Town, Blackburn Rovers and Cardiff City and also host Coventry City and Watford during the month, prior to the Potters coming to the south coast. The two clubs have not met since the 2017/18 season, when both plied their trade in the Premier League.

Leeds United
VERSUS
Southampton

SKY BET CHAMPIONSHIP · MAY 4, 2024

With Saints hoping for an instant return to the Premier League come the end of the 2023/24 season, everyone associated with the club will have their fingers crossed that May 4, 2024 will mark their final match in the Championship for some time.

Saints have not won at Elland Road since March 2012, when a Rickie Lambert goal gave Nigel Adkins' side a 1-0 triumph en route to promotion that season. Russell Martin's team would welcome a repeat result in 2024!

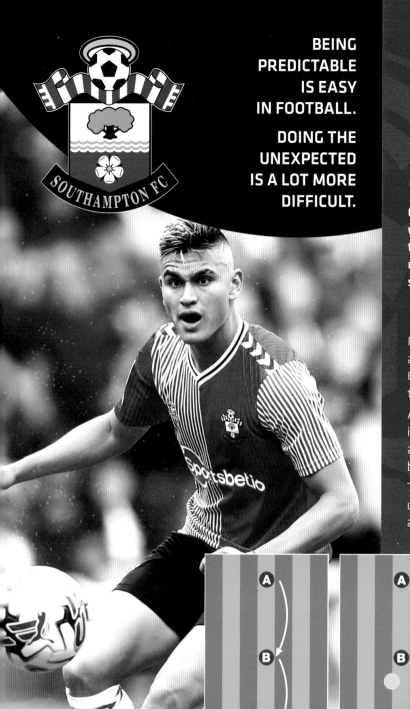

TURNING WITH THE BALL

One of the biggest problems a defence can have to deal with is when a skilful player is prepared to turn with the ball and run at them, committing a key defender into making a challenge. Because football today is so fast and space so precious, this is becoming a rare skill.

EXERCISE 1

In an area 20m x 10m, A plays the ball into B who turns, and with two touches maximum plays the ball into C. C controls and reverses the process. After a few minutes the middleman is changed.

As you progress, a defender is brought in to oppose B, and is initially encouraged to play a 'passive' role. B has to turn and play the ball to C who is allowed to move along the baseline.

The type of turns can vary. Players should be encouraged to use the outside of the foot, inside of the foot, with feint and disguise to make space for the turn.

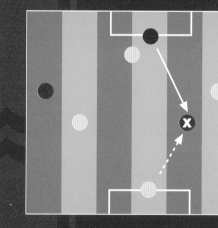

EXERCISE 2

As the players grow in confidence, you can move forward to a small-sided game. In this example of a 4-a-side practice match, X has made space for himself to turn with the ball, by coming off his defender at an angle. By doing this he can see that the defender has not tracked him, and therefore has the awareness to turn and attack.

SOCCER SKILLS

Matches at the top level are won and lost by pieces of skill such as this, so players have to be brave enough to go in search of the ball, and turn in tight situations.

17
STUART
ARMSTRONG

SOUTHAMPTON FC

TEST YOUR
SOUTHAMPTON
KNOWLEDGE
& MEMORY
WITH OUR
HIGH FIVES QUIZ

HIGH FIVES

1. Who have been the Saints' leading league scorers over the past five seasons?

1. _____
2. _____
3. _____
4. _____
5. _____

3. Prior to Russell Martin, who were the club's last five permanent bosses?

1. _____
2. _____
3. _____
4. _____
5. _____

2. Can you name the Saints' last five FA Cup opponents ahead of 2023/24?

1. _____
2. _____
3. _____
4. _____
5. _____

4. Prior to this season, can you name our last five EFL Cup opponents?

1. _____
2. _____
3. _____
4. _____
5. _____

5. Can you recall the Saints' final league position from the last five seasons?

1. _____
2. _____
3. _____
4. _____
5. _____

6. Which members of the Saints' squad started the most league games in 2022/23?

1. _____
2. _____
3. _____
4. _____
5. _____

7. Can you recall these players' squad numbers from the 2022/23 season?

1. Adam Armstrong _____
2. James Bree _____
3. Che Adams _____
4. Carlos Alcaraz _____
5. Moussa Djenepo _____

8. Can you recall the score and season from the last five derby wins over Portsmouth?

1. _____
2. _____
3. _____
4. _____
5. _____

9. Can you remember the Saints' last five Premier League wins from last season?

1. _____
2. _____
3. _____
4. _____
5. _____

10. Can you recall the club's final league points tally from the last five seasons?

1. _____
2. _____
3. _____
4. _____
5. _____

ANSWERS ON PAGE 62

SENSATIONAL
STOPPERS

PETER SHILTON, ANTTI NIEMI AND KELVIN DAVIS WERE ALL GREAT SAINTS SHOT-STOPPERS. CONTINUING THAT PROUD TRADITION IS CURRENT KEEPER GAVIN BAZUNU.

With a crop of bright blonde hair, Antti Niemi cut a very visually distinctive figure between the posts for Southampton for four years. Add in some goalkeeping acrobatics and a famous strike against the crossbar and you've got the makings of a true cult hero.

The Finn struggled with injuries during his time on the south coast, often dipping in and out of the team, but whenever he was fit he offered a big, smothering presence in goal and produced some magnificent saves.

His cat-like reflexes allowed him to pull off some incredible stops from close range against the Premier League's very best strikers.

Peter Shilton's most famous stints in football came in the East Midlands, achieving great things for Nottingham Forest in particular, but Southampton formed an important five-year period in his career as he remained at the top of the game for club and country.

Just shy of 50 of his incredible 125 England caps came while he played for the Saints, where he was voted into the PFA First Division of the Year four years out of five.

He became known across the world for his great reflexes, strong aerial presence and willingness to put his body on the line to claim the ball.

PETER SHILTON

DATE OF BIRTH:	September 18, 1949
PLACE OF BIRTH:	Leicester
NATIONALITY:	English
SAINTS APPEARANCES:	242
SAINTS DEBUT:	August 28, 1982

Southampton 0-1 Coventry City (First Division)

ANTTI NIEMI

DATE OF BIRTH:	May 31, 1972
PLACE OF BIRTH:	Oulu, Finland
NATIONALITY:	Finnish
SAINTS APPEARANCES:	123
SAINTS DEBUT:	September 21, 2002

Southampton 0-0 Charlton Athletic (Premier League)

Davis is a name recognised by generations of Southampton supporters after spending close to a decade between the sticks for the club.

From 2006 to 2013 he made the position his own, sticking with the team as they dropped down into League One and then catapulted back up into the Premier League.

He was selected in the PFA Team of the Year for three straight seasons between 2009 and 2012 as he hit his career-best levels, keeping an incredible 20 clean sheets in the 2010/11 promotion campaign.

Davis made some jaw-dropping close-range stops en route to the top and was a penalty-saving king too!

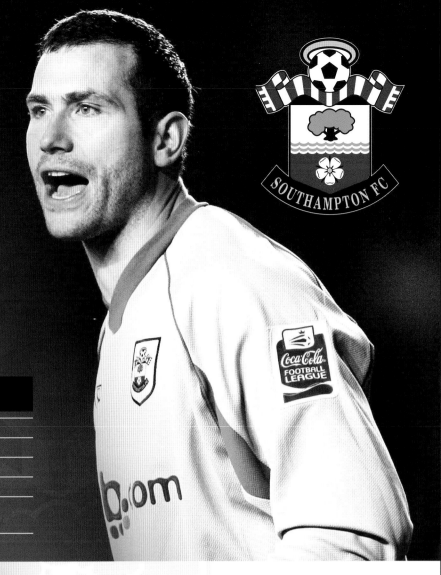

KELVIN DAVIS

DATE OF BIRTH: September 29, 1976

PLACE OF BIRTH: Bedford

NATIONALITY: English

SAINTS APPEARANCES: 301

SAINTS DEBUT: August 6, 2006
Derby County 2-2 Southampton (EFL Championship)

GAVIN BAZUNU

DATE OF BIRTH: February 20, 2002

PLACE OF BIRTH: Dublin

NATIONALITY: Irish

SAINTS APPEARANCES: 37*

SAINTS DEBUT: August 6, 2022
Tottenham Hotspur 4 Southampton 1 (Premier League)

*AS AT THE END OF THE 2022/23 SEASON

Gavin Bazunu is just one year into his Southampton career, and while the first season did not quite go to plan, there's reason to be optimistic about his next steps with the club.

Signed from Manchester City's prolific academy and already a regular Irish international at age 21, Bazunu's modern style of using his feet to good effect and sweeping up behind the defensive line are great fits for the Southampton way and new manager Russell Martin.

He's taken to regular top-level football much earlier than many in his position , meaning there's much still to learn, but plenty to already be excited by.

ANSWERS

PAGE 31: FOOTY PHRASES
Keepie Uppie.

PAGE 34: A-Z QUIZ

A. Austrian. B. Burnley. C. Crystal Palace. D. Derby County. E. Egyptian. F. France. G. Goodison Park (Everton). H. Huddersfield Town. I. Iran. J. Jamaica. K. Kenilworth Road. L. Ladapo, Freddie. M. Middlesbrough (Chuba Akpom). N. Norwegian. O. Oldham Athletic. P. Pukki, Teemu. Q. Qatar. R. Real Madrid. S. Southampton. T. Toffolo, Harry. U. Undav, Deniz. V. Vardy, Jamie. W. Wilson, Ben (Coventry City). X. Xavier, Abel. Y. Yeovil Town. Z. Zenden, Boudewijn.

PAGE 42: FAN'TASTIC

PAGE 45: WHICH BALL
Top: D. Bottom. D.

PAGE 47: SPOT THE DIFFERENCE

PAGE 48: BEHIND THE BADGE

A. Ryan Fraser. B. Samuel Edozie. C. Kyle Walker-Peters. D. Carlos Alcaraz. E. Ryan Manning. F. Stuart Armstrong. G. Will Smallbone. H. Sekou Mara.

PAGE 58: HIGH FIVES

QUIZ 1:
1. 2022/23, James Ward-Prowse (9 goals).
2. 2021/22, James Ward-Prowse (10 goals).
3. 2020/21, Danny Ings (12 goals).
4. 2019/20, Danny Ings (22 goals).
5. 2018/19, Jame Ward-Prowse & Danny Ings (both on seven goals).

QUIZ 2:
1. 2022/23, Grimsby Town (fifth round).
2. 2022/23, Blackpool (fourth round).
3. 2022/23, Crystal Palace (third round).
4. 2019/20, Manchester City (quarter-final).
5. 2018/19, West Ham United (fifth round).

QUIZ 3:
1. Nathan Jones. 2. Ralph Hasenhüttl. 3. Mark Hughes.
4. Mauricio Pellegrino. 5. Claude Puel.

QUIZ 4:
1. Newcastle United, (2022/23). 2. Manchester City, (2022/23).
3. Lincoln City, (2022/23). 4. Sheffield Wednesday, (2022/23).
5. Cambridge United, (2022/23).

QUIZ 5:
1. 20th in Premier League (2022/23). 2. 15th in Premier League (2021/22).
3. 15th in Premier League (2020/21). 4. 11th in Premier League (2019/20).
5. 16th in Premier League (2018/19).

QUIZ 6:
1. James Ward-Prowse (38 Premier League starts).
2. Gavin Bazuna (32 Premier League starts).
3. Kyle Walker-Peters (30 Premier League starts).
4. Mohamed Elyounoussi (27 Premier League starts).
5. Romeo Lavia (26 Premier League starts).

QUIZ 7:
1. 9. 2. 14. 3. 10. 4. 26. 1. 19.

QUIZ 8
2019/20, Portsmouth 0 Southampton 4 (EFL Cup).
2004/05, Southampton 2 Portsmouth 1 (FA Cup).
2004/05, Southampton 2 Portsmouth 1 (Premier League).
2003/04, Southampton 3 Portsmouth 0 (Premier League).
2003/04, Southampton 3 Portsmouth 0 (EFL Cup).

QUIZ 9:
1. Southampton 1 Leicester City 0. 2. Chelsea 0 Southampton 1.
3. Everton 1 Southampton 2. 4. Bournemouth 0 Southampton 1.
5. Southampton 2 Chelsea 1.

QUIZ 10:
1. 2022/23, 25 points. 2. 2021/22, 40 points. 3. 2020/21, 43 points
4. 2019/20, 52 points. 5. 2018/19, 39 points.